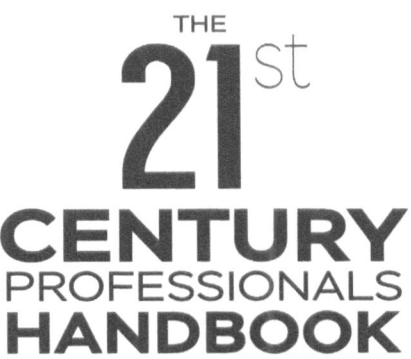

THE
21st
CENTURY
PROFESSIONALS
HANDBOOK

GEN X TO
MILLENNIALS

I0490530

SUVENDU GHOSHAL

INDIA · SINGAPORE · MALAYSIA

Notion Press

No.8, 3rd Cross Street,
CIT Colony, Mylapore,
Chennai, Tamil Nadu – 600004

First Published by Notion Press 2020
Copyright © Suvendu Ghoshal 2020
All Rights Reserved.

ISBN 978-1-64919-955-3

Dedication

This book is dedicated to Baba and Ma. I know you both would have been very happy to see this book published. I miss you. You continue to bless my life and that I write today is because you taught me to do so.

Also to the youthful energy of Millennials which beckons the world, may the world be full of positivity, hope and peace.

Amen

CONTENTS

ACKNOWLEDGEMENTS

I sincerely thank all my colleagues, friends and well-wishers who have encouraged me time to time to do something which I like.

To name a few who pushed me harder than others is Sharmila, my sister. She encouraged me to start writing again and summarise my experience in a book. She has constantly supported me in all my significant life events and as an elder guided wherever I faulted. Being full of follies that is me, full of gratitude to this bonding.

Ishani, my daughter, now a thinking lady, set to launch herself for higher goals, was the biggest support in writing this book. She critiqued, edited, researched visuals for my blog (the original source of the book). I would ask her to do things at short notices for my work and she was always responding. We had tough moments and debates while I was writing but in the end it all turned out well.

Ria, my life partner, gives me the belief which I do not have about myself at times and makes me believe in it and I start believing. At a philosophical level, she is like water to me. Life line, around all the time and comes in when nothing else works. She supported me throughout in this phase of writing and was there to help whenever I reached her. She had also done the mundare job of typing for me, if ever I got tired of the keyboard and never batted an eyelid.

Rajesh Malhotra, my childhood friend has been a great source of encouragement in this journey. He would give feedback on each chapter promptly and share his insights and would encourage me to continue the Millennium series. I will thank him to have kept me motivated in the writing of this book.

Bimal Rath needs a special mention for introducing this book to all of you. A wonderful human being, HR leader and my esteemed colleague helped me in shaping some of my thoughts while discussing 21st Century Manager and that triggered my desire to research more, capture my experiences of working with Senior Leaders and create this book.

I, thank each one of you for making this book happen and also thank the universe for creating a beautiful world which created such powerful experiences for me.

– Suvendu Ghoshal

2020

FOREWORD

The book 'The 21st Century Professionals Handbook – Gen X to Millennials', talks to every professional, especially those in the last couple of workforce generations. With a special focus on Gen X and millennials, the book also highlights the relationships between the different working generations and what to make of them. Whether you are 21 or 45, or anywhere in between, the book can provide some interesting professional insights that can then be converted to action at a personal level. The different chapters all bring fresh perspectives and insights, it is to the reader's imagination, context and goals, as to how best to use these.

A new generation is being shaped through the happenings and awakening around us. One hopes that a more aware, a more sensitive and a more compassionate and balanced generation follows ours. The current pandemic will certainly teach all of us humility, a better sense of dealing with the uncertainties around us and hopefully to be happier with less.

Careers and personal journeys are going to be very different from the past. With changes in technology and societal values, things were already changing rapidly. The younger workforce and especially newer entrants will have to deal with many more variables than the last few generations, where careers were relatively simpler to manage, or at least they got managed pretty much in one single curve. There are three phases as I see it.

Phase I—my father's time: A decent degree, a decent employer and you were set for life.

Phase II—my time: More competition, more opportunities, a little less security but many options if you were ambitious and willing to take some risks.

Phase III—the last 10 years or so: many different opportunities, but not a straight career line any more. Experience may have some value, but increasingly lesser. One could get outdated much earlier than one's retirement age, if not nimble enough. This will possibly hit (and is already hitting) professionals in their late thirties and early forties.

Phase IV –who knows what it will bring: But for certain, the individual and their own self will play a significantly more important role. The better balanced, agile, aware and skilled the individual is, the better the chances of success in life and a career.

This book takes a very holistic look at the phenomenon of young professionals and addresses both the inner world and the outer world of the individual. How they interact, how they overlap, and what the implications are, are all commented upon.

The author's own experiences and wisdom shine through in different parts of the book. The best part of the book is in being both simple to read and understand. It also allows individual readers to form their own impressions while being guided through another set of experiences, some home truths and insights.

Millennial and other young professionals would certainly find value in, especially in building perspectives around a range of topics. The inside out approach to personal pathways, the role of values and relationships, technology and its impact and other aspects are well worth reflecting on.

For me, the most useful and delightful part in the book was about personal choice making, given the uncertainties and many perspectives to be kept in mind. The author keeps coming back to it time and again through the chapters, connecting different dots as they emerge through the narrative.

A nice breezy read for any professional but especially for younger ones, and those getting into the workforce shortly. Happy Reading.

– Bimal Rath

May 2020

INTRODUCTION

Writing a book is a full time job. You have to build a theme around a context and collect and build information around it. You have to believe that there is enough interesting information in it, which can be shared with the readers. You must know that there is a central theme around which each chapter revolves. And importantly each chapter should talk to the other.

To me 'The 21st Century Professionals Handbook' can be a quick reference guide for a more fulfilling professional journey. Through the lens of generations, I have tried to highlight how professionals can work more productively together. I have also tried to examine how care, compassion can make relationships more enriching. While much can be written around the digital world, I have highlighted that illusionary, make believe characteristic of social media impacting gullible millennials.

It all started with my interactions in the business world because of the nature of my job. Thanks to the universe, it gave me knowledge and insights about human mind and behaviour. I came across many assumptions which people gather about each other and how dysfunctional it can become while working together. I also delineated some powerful 'Pet' theories which form the basis of decision making of Professionals – Past,

Present & Future. What prevailed many years ago must rule the future.

After interacting with senior executives through consulting assignments, coaching or leadership interventions and advising innumerable millennials on careers and corporate survival mantra, I would make my notes as part of the coaching reports or significant observation. In parallel, I was reading meaningful literature on Leaders, Baby Boomers, Gen X, Managers and Generation Y, Millennials.

To me defining a 21st Century Manager will not be an easy job. The current occupants of this role are many stakeholders and they bring in unique attributes. There is Gen X, Y on one side, Millennials & Gen Z on the other. They have grown up in entirely different contexts and now they work together. While there are many areas where they demonstrate commonality, yet the uniqueness of these generations stand in contrast.

The values and assumptions between these generations are varied. The way they deal with technology, manage change, approach relationships and navigate work life is very different from each other.

In my leadership workshops or coaching meetings, while I was dealing with some of the common management problems of decision making, skewed communication, relationship challenges, problem solving, goal orientation, I was able to notice certain subtle differences in approach which were generation based. What I mean to say is, if the Manager and his team member belonged to the same generation, the issues will be similar on either side of the table but if they were from two different generations, the problems will be contrasting.

So I thought of creating a 21st Century Professionals handbook on these areas and how to handle the differences. I also wanted to look at 21st Century Professional through the lens of two different generations. I wanted to study how different generations would respond to the same stimulus say in this case, the VUCA (Volatile, Unpredictable, Complex and Ambiguous) world. Or can they be treated the same way i.e., one size fits all or each to their own.

I decided to examine their value system, their behaviours, where does the conflict happen, how can they work together and what needs to change in each one of them or simply put how one understand them better. I also thought that it will be very relevant to understand 21st century in the context of Careers and Gig economy. The following chapters look at this Millennium's professionals with their hopes, aspiration, conflicts and challenges.

It is here that I would also like to mention the challenges we face in the 21st century and how that uniquely positions this century. The rapid pace of change in this century compared to centuries before has picked maximum speed which has kind of become disruptive in nature.

The true significance of globalisation emerged with the 2020 pandemic hitting the whole world together. The world stopped. Global supply chain collapsed and a new order started shaping up. The new mantra being chanted is 'Self-Reliance'. 21st century has seen big businesses collapse overnight, unemployment picking up, social anarchy raising its head and environmental disasters in the making and all in a short time.

I think this century is turbulent. This requires maximum preparedness to lead a fulfilling life and much flexibility in doing that.

Please do let me have your thoughts, feedback and what more could be added for the second edition of this book at suvendu.ghoshal@gmail.com

I hope you enjoy reading this. Happy Reading.

Chapter 1

Case 1

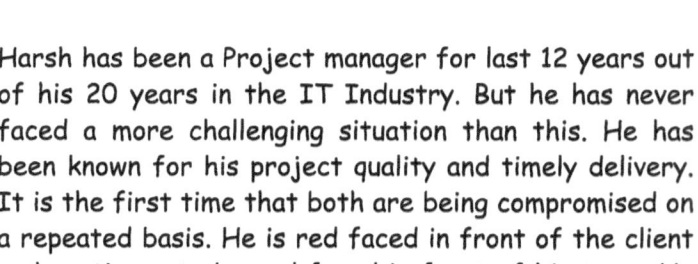

Harsh has been a Project manager for last 12 years out of his 20 years in the IT Industry. But he has never faced a more challenging situation than this. He has been known for his project quality and timely delivery. It is the first time that both are being compromised on a repeated basis. He is red faced in front of the client and continues to be red faced in front of his team. He has had numerous review meetings with his team and has told them how exactly they need to work on this project. But it seems the fairly intelligent, young team has come from another planet and is alien to whatever Harsh is trying to say.

Harsh just concluded a meeting with the Delivery Head wherein the delivery head suggested that since it is a live project, another manager may be deputed to support him. Harsh swallowed his pride and asked for 15 days before they brought in someone else.

Something like this was happening for the first time in Harsh's career. He, being fairly senior, already had one manager supporting him for this Project Team. This project was complex and that is why the best guy was chosen to lead. The team members where hand-picked by Harsh and his Delivery Head basis their pedigree and past performance. They were all from Tier 1 Engineering Institutes and had done very well for themselves in the organization.

In the meetings that Harsh conducted with them, he never experienced any voice of dissent. The only thing he heard in the meeting was silence and meek half compliance to his instructions. He had to quickly identify the problem and solve it.

Q1: What should Harsh do?

Q2: What do you think can be Harsh's problem?

Q3: How should Harsh solve this problem?

EXPERIENCING THE MILLENNIALS, WHERE IS THE CHALLENGE?

We lead most of our lives basis our assumptions; our prejudices decide how we respond to others. Is there actually a generation gap or each generation behaves differently because the context is different. Life taught me that meaning is in the context. To understand others, we just need to understand their context.

> Context defines how you behave

In today's world, the millennials demonstrate a very different mind-set and approach from those professionals who started their career in the 80s or 90s of the 20th century. A different stimulus and a different behaviour. They live in an entirely different world. In the present times the focus has diversified into broader issues like pollution, climate change, plastic, LGBTQ rights and a very inclusive and liberal world.

If we time travel backwards, the focus of Gen X then was to secure a good life for themselves. Today's normal lifestyle of white collar, was aspirational in 20th Century. Black & White Television, Telegram, dial up modem, long queue at the STD booth, just three brands of cars to buy from, air travel only for the top executives, looks like another world and is surreal for the current generation.

The Two Generations Grew up in Very Different Contexts

Let us look at a case from my coaching session to go deeper.

Venu was late for coaching again. I had been waiting for 15 minutes. Being a chartered accountant and being trained in the business world for such a long time, he was always right with his numbers than many other things. Today he got late while completing his coaching log before the session as he shared later.

I looked at his coaching log and it mentioned that he had conducted skip level meetings with his team and he has established deeper connection with them. He was a Vice President in the Treasury Process with an MNC. "So how was your meeting with some associates and Team Leaders," I asked.

'Yes and it was just about okay', said Venu. He was not inclined to verbalise his feeling though his body language said it all.

"Are you not happy meeting them?" I asked.

"No nothing like that. These kids are from a different planet. I am not sure whether they can have a similar long career as we have had" he responded.

"Why do you say so?" I explored with Venu.

"Their responses. Not at all interested in what is happening to the organisation. Only interested in their work". He commented.

"So what"? I provoked him.

"They talk so differently from when I was at same stage. This is what I want, need flexibility in office time, can't get up early, too many reviews and only once in a year reward these are their discussion points, this looks outrageous to me" he was getting angry now.

"Do they deliver work for you" I asked calmly.

"Yes, they do most of the times". He replied.

"Are you not judging them for what they are than their results"? I asked

"What do you mean" like a senior executive he countered me.

I said, "assumptions, my friend", and went on to discuss that.

✳ ✳ ✳

This is one of many conversations, I have had with several Gen X leaders revolving around the same theme. Even if the youngsters give results, many managers have issues about their attitude.

Venu has been dealing basis what he learnt growing up as a professional in 20th Century. He has some assumptions on how to handle a team and he treats them accordingly.

So let's make an attempt to understand what Gen X or Baby Boomers assume when dealing with millennials.

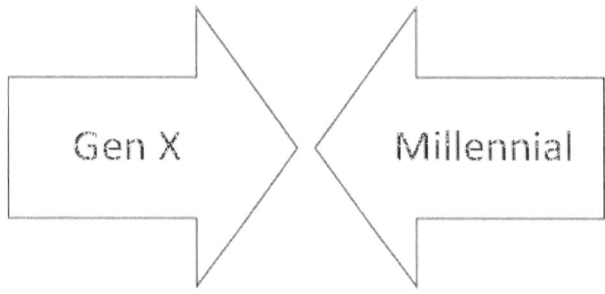

I Have Done It This Way; They Should Do the Same: Assumption 1

If you go with conventional mind set of approaching millennials in the corporate world, you may find it challenging to handle them. What you did when you started your career was relevant in that context. Millennial's response can be outside of the box vis-à-vis programming of Gen X in formative stage of their careers.

Being Generation X, you will look out of sync, if you say that the world has changed since then. It has been transformational. Right from how you are buying stuff, to travelling, to banking, to health management and you can keep adding to it. Even the most core emotion of expressing love has gone digital.

Some businesses have survived, some disappeared and a plethora of new businesses have come up. What remains same is the ingenious human mind of Gen X not wanting to acknowledge this changed reality when they are dealing with the new generation. They seem to expect the same behaviours from them as when they started off. When they don't get that from this generation they are labelled as 'upstarts'.

Expecting Them to Be Compliant the Way You Were Is a Big Fallacy – Assumption 2

When Gen X started, they were expected to be compliant, process driven and just delivering work and if now Gen X is expecting the same from the millennials, they are in for trouble or rather, in no man's land. As a leader/manager, they will find the young workforce as volatile as the market itself. They are neither compliant nor truly process driven but rather goal driven. End result is what matters to them.

They are non-conformist and believe that results justify the means.

The may not bat an eyelid while they jump the rank and deal with your superior directly. Don't blame them for playing politics if the Millennials go to managers superior directly as they don't believe in hierarchy.

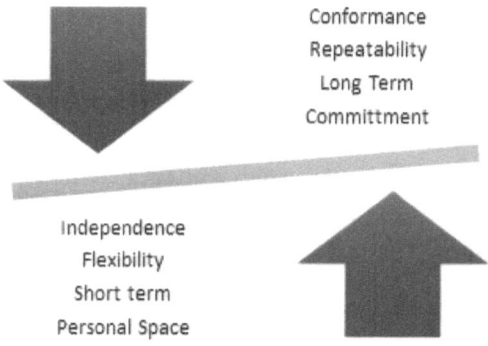

A Good Job Is All That a Youngster Requires – Assumption 3

They might complain about the monotony of the job within a short duration than you would have ever done. They are hungry for doing new things and experimentation. Born in an age of instant gratification, they believe aspirations have a short shelf life and a good job is good for a given time. They are prone to shift their attention to different area as they outgrow a given job.

Performance Reviews Adds to Best Results – Assumption 4

If Gen X reviews the job at short intervals like their superior did with them, Millennials will get frustrated and sulk. They like independence while doing the job and they can't give best results under constant supervision.

They would either reach out to you when they are stuck or when they are in need of expert advice. But, by and large, a Millennial would like to come to you once the job is done. They value their freedom and non-interference in their work.

Expecting Long Term Commitment to the Organization – Assumption 5

Don't assume Millennials will be happy with a promotion if there is no change in Job content like you did. Gen X would be happy with a time bound promotion every 4 years. Millennials may quietly disengage from the job and their manager may not even have a clue.

Gen X was very satisfied when the organisation was comforting and caring and would commit a long innings to it but if you expect the same today from this generation, you are fooling yourself.

The most important aspect for today's millennials is the quality of job first and then anything else. So the commitment to organization is very low and is directly proportional to what the individual is doing.

Do Your Job and You Get Your Salary on Time – Assumption 6

Just doing a job is not the millennials' cup of drink. So if their manager assumes that they have been given a good job and that should be enough. Millennials do not think that way. Gen X was happy just doing a job with a 'no questions asked' attitude. The emerging professionals need clear direction and transparency

Gen Y would be keen to know, what this job will lead them to. Mostly short term in nature, they require clarity on the purpose of work. Sense of boredom sets in Millennials, if they work just like that.

Millennials Need a Manager/Supervisor – Assumption 7

And you thought they would behave the same way as you behaved when your superior walked in....no ways, they respect those who can coach them, guide them and not just manage them.

So as a manager, one gets frustrated not knowing how to deal with them. Your assumptions from the past determine your evaluation of the new professionals. You start giving them names like generation Z, millennials etc. branding them as a different species from yours, not suitable for the world which you have been a part of. The manager promotes the philosophy, values, thinking, systems & processes of a work culture for which there are no listeners.

They Have Arrived and They Are Not Your Clones

The first step in managing change is in recognizing it. Actually as Gen X you don't really have a choice. The Millennials are here and soon they will constitute the largest workforce. Like your desktop changed to tablets & laptops, like your shopping and banking tools became digital and your smart phones replaced your secretary and spouse (figuratively), your next and next generation of corporate professionals have arrived and they look very different from you when you started because the context has changed.

So you can't use the same technique which you learnt from your manager while you are dealing with them.

We have discussed the challenges leaders/managers are facing while dealing with millennials. The way to solve is not to mitigate the problems highlighted but to offer a more comprehensive approach.

For that we need to understand the values of millennials in Chapter 2.

Chapter 2

Case 2

The simmering conflict finally exploded. Ashutosh could not hold on to his anger for Shikha anymore. He burst out saying, 'Shikha there is a way to conduct if you are working. While I acknowledge that you do your job well, there is something called office discipline and', he paused.

'But Sir' said Shikha, she was arbitrarily stopped by Ashutosh, 'let me make my point and please listen'.

'I have been observing you for quite some time and I see that you don't follow the office timings, come late every day, send mails to me and the client in the middle of the night, always with the earplug on while working. If I have to speak to you, I have to shout thrice then only you listen. This is not how we were at your age. Despite you performing well, you need to improve on these aspects' said Ashutosh in one breath.

Shikha heard Ashutosh out and took a deep breath. 'We are a small office and we should make such rules which is convenient to everybody. It seems Ashutosh Sir, you are more concerned about rules than performance. If you think I don't fit in this organization, I will be happy to quit'. Shikha concluded. There was a deadlock and Ashutosh did not know how to handle it.

Q1: What should Ashutosh do?

Q2: Was Shikha right in giving her resignation?

Q3: How would this situation resolve?

THIS IS WHAT I VALUE - MILLENNIALS

Values are your reason for existence, they define you....so here is an attempt to understand values that define the Millennials.

Millennials have grown up in an insecure world. Terrorism, piracy, hacking, viruses both digital and biological started dominating people's life like never before. The world got consolidated with the attack on 9/11. Fear, threat, suspicion, anguish started dominating even positive emotions of life like love, hope and happiness. It shaped the value system of millennials.

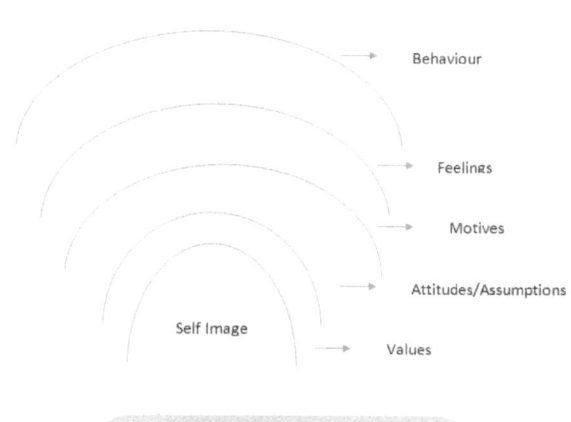

Onion Model of Behaviour

To me, Value is the core around which behaviour revolves. Let's understand values through an onion. The top most layer is behaviour. As we peel off the 1st layer, the second layer is feelings, like when we feel good (feeling), we smile (behaviour) or when we are sad (feeling), we cry (behaviour) etc.

If we peel the layer of feelings, the next layer is of Motive which means only if I get a certain stimulus, I feel happy or sad and behave accordingly. I may score 98% in 12th and still not be happy as my motive is to top the board.

Below the layer of motive is attitude, a semi quasi time bound disposition of mind towards anything - like your attitude when in college is different from your attitude in school. In school it is conformism, homework, wishing teachers, restricted movement whereas college it is care free, independence based.

The last layer is of values. Deep and enduring over a significant period in one's life. Values get formed in the formative years of life. Apart from the universal value of love, honesty, courage, help – Value is what you value.

> Personal values gets influenced by the times we are living in

One can value success, another can value money and a third can value fun. To each their own but definitely influenced by the times we are living in.

A Deliotte survey of 2019 highlights that Millennials are low on trust and optimism.

Hence a low commitment to long term career with one organisation or settling in with one partner.

Hence a low commitment to long term career with one organisation or settling in with one partner

Trust deficiency or pessimism has direct correlations with the times they have been brought up. Another significant value for this generation is of equality, hence there is a high pitched voice for social justice which we hear from this generation, be it LGBTQ or #Me-Too or the Underprivileged.

Bag pack traveller is a term associated with this generation. They will work for few days and take time out for travel. Millennials are very particular about their 'Me Time'.

Millennials are better team players than other generations because one of their significant values is diversity. They accept each other as they are and do not judge them.

More spiritual than religious

If Gen X triggered acceptance of rational thinking over faith as a way of life, millennials are championing it. Rooted to the value of empiricism, they are more spiritual than religious. The faithlessness in dogmatic religion can lead to the obituary of many customs and rituals associated with religion and also in moments of weakness, the millennials may lose hope faster than their previous generation due to the absence of strong religious practise in their life. The millennials need to think this over.

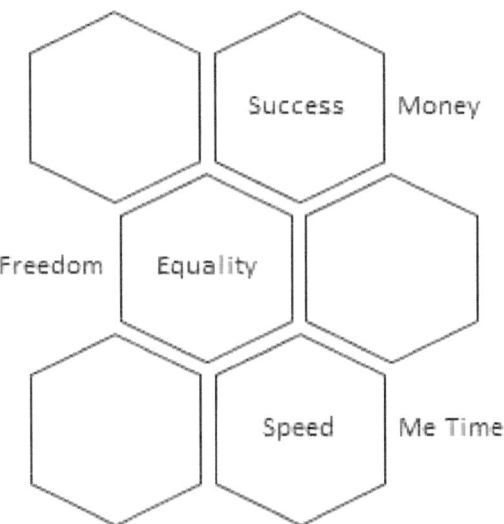

Interestingly research shows that Millennial's are passionate about values. A Gallup survey points that Millennials push for change (behaviour) consistently because of their value system: a) on being unattached and b) free flowing (unconstrained).

Another of their core value is living in 'here & now' and one of the outcome of it is promoting consumerism and short term future orientation.

The value of learning (ansuya) is integral to Millennials. This value makes Millennials better prepared to handle the chaotic world (vikriti) of the present.

Compare this with Gen X, when they were growing up, the world was less chaotic, digital world far away, face to face relations were the only relations, today's necessities were luxuries then. In those times, people would go to others house to make a phone call or watch TV together.

Trust, hope, aspirations were more strong in the past than cynicism, despondency and faithlessness of the present. Religious festivals were occasions for community gatherings than celebrating individualistic father's day, mother's day, friendship day, daughter's day etc under the influence of globalisation.

So Gen X is by and large more optimistic and more vulnerable to trust easily. Their values anchor around stability, permanence, faith, conformance. They will not break the chain of command and follow the hierarchy. Family will always be preferred over being single.

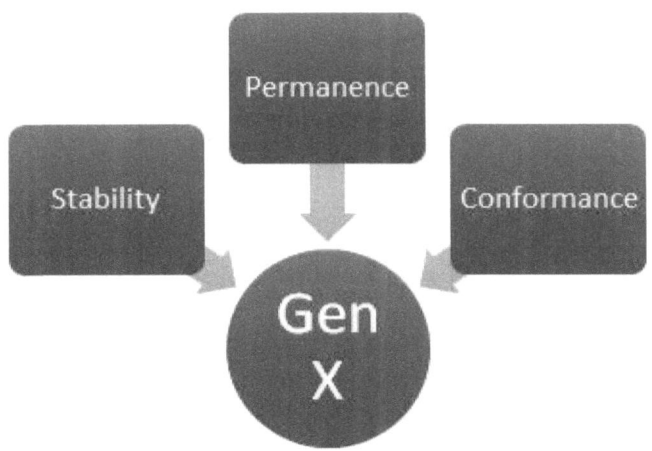

Gen X believe that respect elders irrespective of what value they create unlike Millennials who believe that respect is to be given to those deserving and they are not hierarchy driven. For Gen X, stability will mean they will buy houses and create other assets for themselves and secure their family.

> Understand values to know why they behave
> the way they behave

If we are able to understand the value systems of different generations, one will know why they behave the way they behave. The chaos or disorder that gets created when two different generations take on each other can get minimised if we understand each other's world. Lot of bad breath, negative energy can be proactively eliminated.

Also if we are able to appreciate values as something deeper and more permarent than anything else, then our acceptance of each other becomes lot simpler. Managing, dealing with millennials or Gen X can work through the path of Values.

Chapter 3

Case 3

Rachna is in an assessment center. This was mandatory in her organization for career advancement. Here she is aspiring for the next level as Associate Vice President. She is to write an essay about her observations on fresher's.

She described them as someone with a headphone, always glued to their smart phone and more interested in Instagram than Facebook and commitment averse. They understand the latest in technology.

Q1: Do you think Rachna gave a comprehensive response to the question?

Q2: How will you describe today's youngster's?

WE ARE MILLENNIALS

As you approach to talk to a millennial at their workstation, you may have to take their name twice as they will be sitting in front of a laptop with their headphones acting as a shield from the immediate world. In between, they will pick up the phone to connect with the digital world through WhatsApp, Instagram, Snapchat etc. That's generation Z, very much connected, responding in their new way and definitely, not your way.

They work hard, party hard, focus on producing the best results, analytics, delivery or sales

Welcome to the World of Millennials!

Millennials' use of digital technology clearly sets them apart. One of the defining characteristics of the millennial generation is their affinity with the digital world. They have grown up with broadband, smartphones, laptops with social media being the norm and expect instant access to information.

- A report from PWC.com

This is the first generation to enter the workplace with a better grasp of key digital business tools than their senior workers. This generation rather grew up with it.

So What Is the DNA of Millennials?

Digital warriors with headphones as a symbolic metaphor.

Yet, Millennials get a bad reputation for this. Gen X often view them as lazy, glued to their smart phones or gadgets and not willing to actually work hard to achieve workplace success. Often described as the "generation of entitlement" or the "I want it now" generation, they are the defining generation for the fast moving present and fast catching up future.

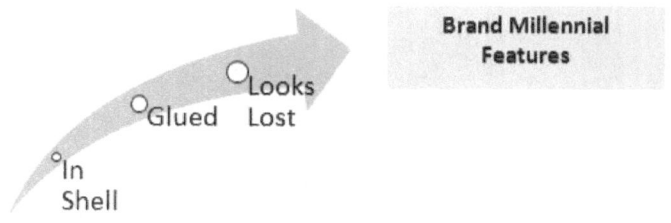

More Individualistic

Driven by a highly consumer oriented society, they want more out of life, rather, more out of everything. They invest more in self, whether self-development or enjoyment. While protecting Me, Mine and Myself, they hold similar views for others, egalitarian in values, tolerant of others, they will embrace house help or women leaders as equal more easily than others.

They are more open to taking risks and will walk into new experiences. Driven by more social awareness, they are open to consultation with peers and seniors alike.

Don't Beat Around the Bush Please....

Asim regretted in one of the coaching discussions that he was unable to clearly communicate the work from home policy in a face to face meeting with a super achiever. He used the subtle way which he had learnt many years ago. He went through indirect channel to convey that message to the person. The message was; work from home is an exception than a norm. The result, the person did not appreciate this approach and left within a month and Asim lost a bright resource.

They prefer straight heart to heart talking, no song and dance communication. Millennials want blunt, clear and concise messaging. Ambiguity bothers them and they have an inherent dislike towards hypocrisy.

Want to Fly High

In a world primarily belonging to the self and a positive self-image, the goals are lofty and maybe surreal at times. Filled with high aspirations, millennials are prone to job change for faster growth. They are ambitious, knowledgeable, more exposed to the world through digital platforms. They are aware that there are many success stories where individuals have become billionaires even before they have hit 30's. They also know success can come to anyone just not to those with good pedigree. One has to work towards it relentlessly. They are true iconoclasts.

I was mentoring an IIT, Kanpur 4ᵗʰ year student. Our discussion was around how he can create a self-management strategy to support his business plan. He was a serial entrepreneur and doing all of that himself. What I gathered that he had set few clear personal goals before entering thirties and he expected one of his enterprise to hit the bulls eye and make him a billionaire.

They desire nothing less than being the top performer, the master of the game. And the super achievers work very hard for it.

Yes, there is a flip side to it. If Millennials don't get what they want, one of the fall out is negative emotion. In many conversations with youngsters that I have had they have expressed their desire to be a manager in a short time. Not everyone is a super achiever and surely a wishful thinking. So long term goal setting is not a regular practice with most.

It is either a dream or a perceived positive outcome and if it's not achieved, then there is a deep disillusionment. The outcome of the same is depression, anxiety and mood swings. They get disconnected from the prevalent reality much faster than Gen X.

> The millennials may be more prone to have negative feelings in case of failure

I Work to Live

If generation X talked about work life balance, the millennials practise it. It is very important for millennials to lead a high quality life. Fancy gadgets, good clothes, good vacations and good food. You may experience the split persona in this generation. While some of them you will find lazy and extremely sedentary. They are happy as long as they appear fit to a labouring health freak who loves a good body.

It is one life that you must live fully.

Work From Anywhere

But that is where the beauty lies, being virtual life mongers, they bring huge flexibility and give solutions to work situations virtually from anywhere. They don't have to walk into their work stations to start working. They work from everywhere.

Working from anywhere also frees their spirit and their sense of independence. The autonomy that it provides makes them take charge of work. With clarity on what to do, they focus on here and now.

Ask them about future, they will give you a wry smile. No wonder real estate is not doing well for quite some time. They will outsource housing, furniture, food while they focus on what they enjoy most.

Being Focused on the Present

Living in the present can be stressful to Gen X. They are trained to do future proofing. Buy a house, buy insurances, save for rainy day etc. For millennials, present is what matters and they are literally cool about rest of the things. They find it mundane. Live on rentals, be bag pack person, feed and grow self.

This throws few challenges to the millennials. They are not long term planners and cannot think far ahead, often missing the big picture. While their risk taking ability brings in an impulsive response to a situation, they may be challenged in deep cognitive thinking. It is just that they have not practised that not enough.

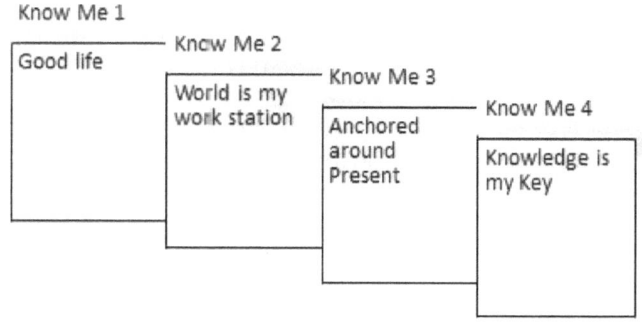

Being the First to Share

Being continuously digitally connected, they are lot more aware of international and national affairs or events than others. They are on Twitter, Instagram and other sites and are continuously updated and you will seldom get the opportunity to break a news to them. They will always be the first.

History of time is a witness, different civilizations contributed to the growth of humanity uniquely. Each generation in a civilization exhibit some unique characteristics. There may be some overlap with the past and future generation but each generation has sharp differentiators.

During the times of Industrial revolution, people demonstrated thriftiness, hard work and discipline to name a few. This is the time of digital revolution, where artificial intelligence, big data analytics have started doing complex human activities. Time is not far away when Alexa starts responding to your emotions. Alexa I am feeling sad and it starts playing a mood changing music or reads my body language and responds. And millennials are in the middle of all this. They are creating it, they are using it and upgrading it. That's their uniqueness.

Chapter 4

Case 4

Tushar was at his wits end thinking about Sarthak and his team. It seemed that Sarthak had a magic wand. His team had the best feedback from clients, lowest attrition, highest productivity, absence of conflict and great team work. In fact, it was very difficult for Tushar, a more senior person in the organization than Sarthak, to get anybody from Sarthak's team to his team. Rather, he had got many requests from his team to move to Sarthak's team. He did not know what spell Sarthak had cast on his team.

Tushar decided to speak to Sarthak to address few of his immediate problems. His team was to deliver a critical client project of high importance shortly and he needed some members from Sarthak's team to come and join him. Sarthak spoke to Tushar for good half an hour after Tushar gave a commitment to take Sarthak's peer feedback objectively and without any malice.

Sarthak told Tushar that he had received some feedback about Tushar's way of working from the young workforce revolving around his communication style, his attitude towards youngsters, his way of engaging junior team members and the prevalent culture of matrix driven performance review.

Tushar made a note of all the points and said to Sarthak that he will try to work on this feedback while dealing with youngsters.

Q1: Make a list of behaviours which will work well with a young team.

Q2: If you were Tushar what action plan you would create?

GEN X - THE WINNING STRATEGY

A survey by Deloitte shows that more than 40 percent of millennials expect to leave their jobs within two years and fewer than 30 percent want to be in the same job for more than five years. The same Deloitte survey shows that millennials value and are most willing to stick with companies that have diverse management teams and flexible work environments.

The Millennial generation – the group of people who were born after 1980's, or largely grew up in the 2000s and know nothing about rotary telephones, dial-up modems or even having just three or four television channels.

Obviously Gen X cannot adopt the 'one size fits all' management style for this generation. What they developed as leadership style or saw their managers practise needs to be re-examined while they deal with the completely new millennial achiever.

And knowing how to handle, manage, motivate millennials to get best business results matters most today. This is the generation which is going to take over the workforce in a very, very short amount of time.

You see, those "children" are becoming adults now. According to Fromm of Forbes, this generation will make up roughly 75 percent of the workplace by 2030. This means the Baby Boomers and Generation X- are going to be pushed out in the very near future.

So for Leaders/Managers what is my change mantra to best appreciate millennials and co-work with them?

> By 2030 – 75% Of workforce will be
> of Millennials

Understand Their World

Know how they learn, how they gather knowledge, how they achieve, how they make decisions, how they socialize and things that are important to them. Also you should know what is irrelevant, what does not matter to them like discussing religion may not be a good choice. For them religion is a personal choice and a very private affair. Find out what is unimportant to them which overlaps into the Gen X world like respect for hierarchy vis-a-vis respect for talent. Know the gap and create a plan to deal with it.

Recognize Them as Digital Leaders

After the collapse of communists and emergence of a free market, the next big sweep is the digital revolution. It is impacting all aspects of life and this generation of millennials are born with a tablet. They understand technology and its usage better than most. They can lead you in this area.

It's a joke with senior leaders that how poor they are in understanding technology; they do understand the benefits of digitization but do not know how it happens. Most of the time, Gen X after giving the client requirement for automation to their IT partner or vendor do not understand much when the requirement gets converted in a technical report. That's where a new generation millennial can play an impactful role.

Millennials not only know about technology but are also aware of global practices. Gen X will find it useful to coronate them as digital leaders, by keeping them in the forefront of all digital projects or activities.

Micromanage and Doom Yourself

Give Millennials the long rope after delegating work. You have to be patient and trust them that they will deliver. They will not disappoint you. They will give you results.

Amit is a typical ESTJ manager. He climbed the corporate ladder through delivery excellence. Known globally for his project management skills. Goals, planning, implementation, review and control were his known competencies. Since last one year he has been facing the challenge of attrition. While he continued to deliver high quality projects but his reputation had taken a hit. And he was blaming the youngsters for bad mouthing.

Actually his skip level team members were saying that they do not get the independence in their work. His style represented control orientation with a high need to know and he was encountering the silent rebellion in the team and only few people were vocal about.

Empower Millennials, agree to a target with them and leave them to deliver. They prefer reaching their managers when they are stuck or need advice.

Empowering junior staff is difficult aspect to implement for the senior managers, it means creating a very strong need for internal change, and simultaneously accepting the new reality and adopting a more flexible aspect to deal with millennials.

willing to let go and not control

Ground Rule of Communication

Keep it simple, precise and straight!

Millennials are not used to vague discussions. Keep talks esoteric or high level and you may get a mute participation from them.

Tolerance for ambiguity in communication is not very high with millennials. They are the binary generation of 0s or 1s. They look for concreteness in discussions when it comes to work planning or delivery and they show 100% commitment in achieving it. There are occasions where they have asked clients to be specific in the presence of a Gen X leader. When you ask them later 'Why did you do this with the client', they are clear in their response, 'Because I have to deliver it'.

Senior Managers have shared that they get great results when they have made precise communication while allowing juniors to deliver freely.

Flexibility in Attitude Will Get Best Results From Millennials

Millennials binge. They will finish a Netflix web series just sitting at one place and they do the same with work. Place of work for them is notional. They work from anywhere and deliver great results. So working from home should not be a big deal. A typical 9 to 5 work schedule need not be changed but do show a lot of flexibility around that to get best productivity from them.

This may require shift in attitude from process to results and productivity and Gen X may require some time to get entrenched in the culture, though this pandemic of 2020 has shown them the way.

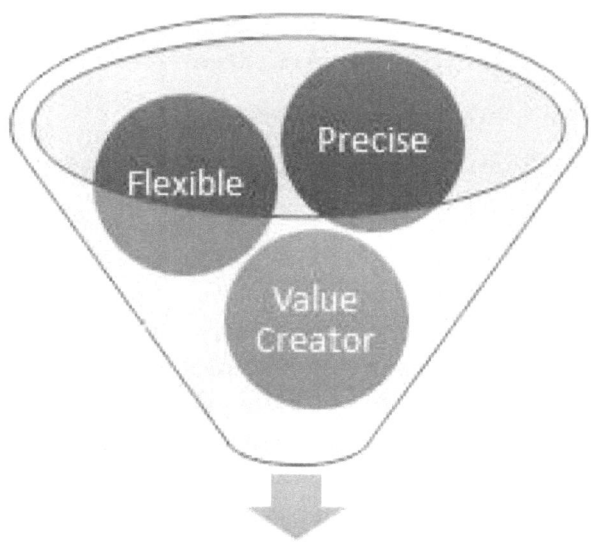

Millennial's Stimulus

Be a Collaborator & Promote Diversity

Create systems and practices where team members succeed together, individual members do not matter. As long as they work together to produce results. Millennials work with an open mind. They collaborate with their colleagues in the virtual world as much as the physical world. They are comfortable working with any gender, colour or ethnicity. They do not hold any bias.

Youngsters that I speak with on work by and large demonstrate an open mind, willing to embrace all useful things to become productive. Know that Millennials are great collaborators and are confident about themselves. This is the single most differentiator which gives them the strength to not feel insecure with others or threatened. The more diverse the team, the more they get engaged as it creates new learning.

Gen X can create processes to support inclusivity and collaboration. They will get better business results from the youngsters.

> Millennials are confident about self

Recognize the Achievements

Create meaningful work for millennials and facilitate them to succeed. Acknowledge the success. Research shows that new generation has two significant requirements. One, a constant need to do something new and two, a constant need to be recognised for what they are contributing.

They have a high need to achieve and a hunger for recognition. They see no recognition in mundane and routine work, hence shun such opportunities after a point in time.

If the senior leaders address this requirement of millennials they need to consciously create exciting opportunities for Millennials. This is doable for business as it will create more intrapreneurs, new enterprise. It will also strengthen Gen X in business & their functions. It's a win-win.

More a Coach & Mentor Than a Manager

In my several interactions with Managers, I have discovered that successful managers not only deliver great results but they also have outstanding relation with their teams. They are great listeners. They are full of compassion and empathy and influence others through their behaviours.

Millennials are always inspired by influencers than managers. Gen X must know the difference between being a manager and being a coach. Don't start solving problems for them, which typically a manager does. Be a coach by asking questions about the problem and generating options with them, let them choose the answer. Connect with them at their level and not where you operate from.

> Gen X will still have empowering power and expert influence

Senior Managers may not find this very easy to implement. As a manager you are used to giving instruction. There is power and authority associated with it. Well, if you can take the difficult journey of transitioning to a coach, it will be worth the effort. You will still have empowering power and expert influence. It will also free up your time and increase resourcefulness in the team.

Gen X have to be inventive while working in 21st Century. Individual values, work systems, work culture all of these have undergone major changes in this millennium. To address that, Gen X have to do a calibration of the work practices they have learnt or the work culture when they started working. Clients/customers have very high expectations. They have so many options to choose from and so do the employees. Old tricks will not work in a new playing field.

Chapter 5

Case 5

In the past fortnight, every time you would walk up to Ishita to greet her you will find her with swollen eyes and strips of medicine lying on her work station. As a manager, Shekhar had already got used to her coming late because she would do her work in the night and deliver work for him. But apparently in the last 15 days, her productivity had slipped drastically.

Shekhar thought it is time for him to have a talk with her. He called her and while they were sitting in the meeting room, Ishita presented a very stoic face. When Shekhar confronted her with a straight question on what is happening in her personal life, Ishita put forward a brave face and said that she was having some relationship challenges with her husband. Shekhar expressed his surprise by stating that they had a courtship for more than 2 years and now married for a year, so what happened, all of sudden.

To this Ishita responded by saying that he is a nice guy and comes from a good family but her compatibility quotient with him is poor. Shekhar probed. She responded by saying that he is too judging and very closed about my 'Me Time'.

'Of late our disagreements have become more vocal and at times violent. I have no choice but to visit a psychiatrist and take lot of drugs to get a good night sleep. I know I have been erratic at work and also missing some deadlines. I think I am going for a separation and soon I will bounce back', Ishita said blankly.

Shekhar advised her to proceed on leave till such time.

Q1: What do you think is Ishita's problem?

Q2: Did Shekhar give her the right advice?

THE MILLENNIAL'S DILEMMA – ET TU, BRUTE

Being vulnerable is a big stress factor for millennials. When a friend speaks the truth which is painful, they find it as betrayal. This generation is not prepared to accept, skilled to handle and purposeful to mitigate pain or bitter truth.

Research shows that millennials ability to handle shock, setbacks is distinctly lower than the previous generation. They slip fast into depression if they find reality different from what they thought. They also have short term goals, and thus are unprepared for a long journey. A long journey always trains people about good, bad, ugly situations.

In this chapter, we are going to explore some key skills or competencies millennials need to acquire to deal with themselves and world better. Let us look at some of the challenges they have.

Developing Meaningful Relationships – Challenge 1

Call it commitment phobia or anything else, the gen Y & Z are best when the relationship is at a 'cool' level. It is not demanding. They are happy with the 'likes' that they get in the digital world. At work, interaction with colleagues is to deliver work and it seldom develops into strong bonding. Office parties are described as good fun. More often than relationship are defined by terms like 'hang out' or 'make out'. To be a brave at heart and commit to a long term relationship is decreasing in popularity in the current times.

BRAVE
– AT –
Heart

This increasing social atrophy is a grave concern for sociologists. This threatens the traditions & customs associated with religion or community like Dushera celebrations, Shiva Ratri or picnics and so many such positive community gatherings. These customs may fade with the exit of Gen X.

Meaningful relations and Community binding are two such areas this new generation may have to consider to look at consolidating for sake of positivity, family and community.

To commit, care and understand another person's world is a challenge which millennials must meet. It does not end with the established position that a millennial takes that they respect and accept every one for what they are. And after that you live your life and I live mine. They need to examine this assumption. They need to go deeper.

There is enough evidence of the collateral damage that happens in the absence of commitment to a relation. They need to have vertical integration both above and below to stop that trend. Because if we look at civilization vertical integration has helped in maintaining harmony, care and concern with partners, peers and friends.

If they want to be real leaders, they have to build real relations, connect with people's heart. Millennials need to show their intellect and thinking in person. Indeed, they may not have large audience as in the virtual world but this is another world, equally important.

And in this self-fulfilling prophecy, they at times become oblivious to certain profound issues or the innate bond of people. Millennials ultimately rule the world of instant gratification, whereas it is will worthwhile for them to mull over deeper philosophies, values and other significant aspects of life like family, long term commitment and trust.

The Real World Social Person – Challenge 2

While Millennials live and spend more time in a virtual world, their digital social skills are well-groomed. In a world of likes & dislikes, friending and unfriending, emojis and new lingo, they make their digital social presence felt. They are experts in digital conversations, following digital trends, trolling and viral bombing, they are the key board warriors, a new form of warfare increasingly prevalent now.

Here is another case for you to consider.

Rashmi was crying inconsolably. She was having a release in her coaching session. Reason her good friend and colleague had bad mouthed about her. The result, a loss of opportunity for onsite transitioning. "Are you sure?" I asked. "Yes, very much, my team leader himself shared this, he further told Shaila had shared that in my last onsite assignment, how I got drunk after a party and embarrassed the whole team from India. Its partially true as others also got drunk". Rashmi said in one breath.

Do you think Rashmi was owning her problem?

✳ ✳ ✳

There will be many Rashmis around, who don't know how to handle tough situations in reality. They are comfortable to deal with different social media platforms.

Yet, at a gathering cutting across professionals and generations, they struggle to demonstrate their real world social skill. They struggle to make conversations or have long discussions. Having spent long hours in the digital world they are very well trained in that domain but have less practise of face to face social skills. They have not devoted enough time learning real social protocols and norms.

They must practise sweet nothings in communication. Make conversations just like that in real situations. Initiate interesting discussions. Perhaps create a long to-do list to make their social presence felt like a personal call or meeting than a text message or initiating religious tradition at home, etc.

At the click of a button, in an increasingly consumer driven society, the millennials have acquired awesome power to control their own life, if not others. They may learn, reflect and change, only if they are sure about a significant personal result.

Gen X also gets governed by the self-felt need to change but under a larger social umbrella. In the case of millennial, is the umbrella missing?

> Real leaders come from the real world and not from the black screen of your mobile phones.

Living in a Make Believe World – Challenge 3

Instagram, Snapchat, WhatsApp, Facebook is a world which gen Y, Z consciously creates for themselves, they live and curate that world. Millennials want people to know them in a given way.

Some go overboard and start promoting themselves through photo shopped looks, filters and borrowed thoughts.

This projection of their self, creates an illusionary world for themselves. Some millennials live in that illusion.

They start believing the interactions on the social media as real ones and all the adulation received in those platforms as the only truth. This may be very different from what the actual reality is. This leads to a distorted self-image and self-esteem, disconnected from their real self. Any negative stroke from the virtual world leads to anxiety, loneliness, dejection and misery. This is despite all attempts by family & friends to show solidarity and positivity.

> There is a growing trend of depression, anxiety being caused as a direct outcome of the internet world

Millennials need to understand how the digital world operates and calibrate their expectations accordingly. Certain likes or popularity of some meme/videos is totally culture driven in the internet platforms. Some in this generation will do better to appreciate cultural differences between regions along with taking a part of life and not whole of it.

The social quotient of any one is just not through digital world alone. While the digital world is here to stay, millennials need to step up and go beyond that and add more friends beyond close circle. Creating a balance between both the worlds.

Beyond the Digital World: The Real Communication – Challenge 4

I always tell participants in my coaching program that if one is doing small things well than planning for a big one, there is always a higher possibility of success. Millennials can start by meeting or picking up the phone to greet people personally and directly on different social and festive occasions than sending a WhatsApp message.

Make small conversations whenever surrounded by people. Keep making mental notes on how many times you have reached out to others and made conversations. Take off your head phones and listen to the sound of the nature. Enjoy a bird chirping or the gentle swish of air rustling the leaves of a tree, the pitter patter of rains.

Try to interact in reality with the chaos of the society. Listening and responding in reality is an emotional experience for the sender and the receiver.

All this will mean real communication in the real world.

Self Before Business – Challenge 5

Me, mine, myself at times takes precedence over anything else. So many millennials may think customers, client can wait, but in reality customers don't wait, they have other options.

I need to take off, work can wait attitude can be counterproductive for some of them. While their own goals are important, they must also have top priority for super-ordinate goals of the business. After all they are here because of the business, the customers.

> Create balance between personal goals
> and work Goals

Seeing the Big Picture – Challenge 6

Am I able to visualise a scenario five years from now. Most millennials will say 'No' and reason out by saying that it is too far off. Going beyond the present and near future is a challenge which the millennials must address.

To have a long term view of where they want to see themselves, will make them resourceful and experts in their field. It will also help them to take informed decisions not just for work but for their self too. While transactions are handled on a short term basis but any big impact, invention, philosophy always requires a long term commitment.

Having the big picture also prepares the millennials to deal with obstacles far better.

Knowing their True North and setting life goals will help Millennials to step outside the world of instant gratification and create balance between long term and immediate goals and thus making them more purposeful.

The moment one is able to see the big picture, this develops the ability to connect the dots of the present and draw synergy and reduce misalignments and create a plan for future travel.

Critically Think – Challenge 7

Millennials practise linear thinking and think straight. It helps them to stay focussed. 21ˢᵗ Century appears more like a maze with its disrupting power.

In these times, Generations need to develop further the ability of critical thinking and not look at things at face value. Expand lateral cognitive process and you will have multiple options.

The world of internet has answers to everything in this galaxy. Unfortunately, millennials and us, we all believe that those are the only answers. But it is far from the truth.

There is a deeper world unfortunately not easily accessible on the internet, millennials need to go there, develop critical insights and contribute with proficiency. A researcher's mind-set and farmer's toil is the combination they require to go beyond the basics.

These are some thoughts on how millennials can become more effective as they prepare to become and subsequently lead the workforce in the 21ˢᵗ Century.

Chapter 6

Case 6

Raja had decided to be self-employed after spending 22 years in the corporate world. When he started he was able to leverage his network of professional friends but after couple of years he found the work drying up.

Pranav a youngster with 3 years of experience decided to be an entrepreneur at an early stage of his career. At about the same time as Raja had spent, Pranav's entrepreneurship had taken off and he had employed a four-person team to support in his business enterprise. One of the advantage which Pranav had over Raja was his digital literacy.

Raja had heard the term Gig working but never made an attempt to understand how it operates. He was still using conventional means of sending mass SMS and mailers, cold calls and tapping his network. All this was giving Raja limited returns.

Q1: What do you think Pranav would have done right to promote his business?

Q2: What more Raja could do to revive his fading business in the Gig culture?

GIG ECONOMY IN THIS MILLENNIUM

The significance of this chapter in this book is to throw open an interesting work option which has emerged for professionals. Secondly to highlight how this new emerging sector works. If one has to go and work there, what attitude, skills and expertise one needs.

So here it goes, Millennials and Gig economy seamlessly blend into each other. Millennials love their independence, value short work commitments, may have most unorthodox career and gig economy provides them the plug & play platform.

What Is a Gig Economy?

Gig is a term used in music identified by a single performance by a composer. The same analogy has been used to define an economy based on temporariness. Where employment is short term and project based. And you only get the projects based on your expertise and not on your experience. In a gig economy you can work on many projects at the same time with multiple clients.

Growing rapidly, this phenomenon is fast catching up with India. Close to 150 million workers in US and Europe have left the relatively stable confines of corporate life — sometimes by choice, sometimes not — to work as free lancers, increasingly adding to the strength of Gig workforce.

Apart from transaction-oriented service platforms, a recent report by Mckinsey highlighted that knowledge-intensive industries and creative occupations are the largest and fastest-growing segments of the freelance economy.

> *Knowledge workers are the key component in a Gig economy*

The "gig economy" is altering the way that people view and perform work, and countries must be ready to respond with innovative policies and programs to deal with this new wave of employment of a different kind.

Roots From the Past

Every summer my driver would take a month off and go to his village for harvesting. He would reap the crop, polish it and take it to the mandi, sell it and prepare for the next harvest. At times he would extend his vacation depending on the harvest.

Most of the migrant workforce out of Nation Capital Region of India would follow a similar pattern of project based employment depending on where and what kind of work is there. This labour class prefers temporariness in their work as it gives them flexibility to pick and choose work and the time. This trend in the labour market has been in vogue for a long time.

Driver, Carpenter, Painter, Mason, Plumbers, Maids etc have been leading this life since the growth of urbanisation. Now there is a similar pattern happening with their employers and they are being called as gigers.

Why It Works So Well With the Business

There has been a growth of the service sector and saturation in traditional manufacturing jobs. Heavy industry with large factories are more conducive to stable, full-time work and it has been relatively stagnant. In business the focus has shifted to creating customer demand and increase sales and hence there is an increasing emphasis on servicing the customer. The norm in service sector is more on outcome than on process. Hence, the ever-growing service sector, interestingly, is more conducive to flexible part-time work and short-term contracts.

The Virtual Platforms

The internet enables many people to work from home and deliver the same or better service than large corporates. It also has the advantage of being less expensive. For example, there is a rise in the number of people working as online project managers, independent consultants, software developers. The aggregators have really made it easy for the customers as they have eliminated the filter of big business houses and deliver a faster and high quality service.

> Websites such as Upwork, eBay, Etsy, Noble House etc have facilitated this economic diversity

Shift in Economy

In a VUCA world, the market, the customer, the seller shifts overnight. Disruptors of the market are here to stay and businesses prudently want to manage their finances while delivering to clients. They want to invest only where it is absolutely necessary. So project based work or gig workers suit them better than having permanent workforce on their roles.

Fewer Resources Needed

With the workforce being gig-based and working remotely, the businesses don't have to invest a lot of money on creating infrastructure and providing for retirals, bonuses, attractive perks and healthcare etc. This works as a big plus for businesses to look for project based engagement and reduce manpower cost.

No Expenditure on Training

Large business houses end up spending huge money on employee development. It kick-starts with an employee's joining and goes on a continuous basis in the career of an employee. Since the gig worker is already an expert in their own field, the businesses don't have to spend on their training as well and at the same time they have the flexibility to use them on need basis.

A senior project manager in an IT maintenance firm said 'We get some brilliant specialists for our designing work, they are costly but the other overheads are not there - no training costs, no annual benefits etc, our own team is only doing the routine jobs.'

Expert Pool

You don't have to groom, nurture and develop experts. Businesses get to appoint Experts at their work for their work. There is also an indirect result apart from reducing development cost. This reduces office politics and corridor talks, leading to increase in productivity and high quality service and unlike employees, experts doing this do not treat it as just another job.

For the economy, it shows better employment numbers as the self-employed are added to it. In UK, employment has gone up by 12% as also by more than 15% in US and other European economies.

What's in it for Millennial white collar workers

'I want to be Me' said Daksh, a dynamic IIT grad from batch 2019. 'So what's the plan?' I asked. 'Want my own start up'. Here he was representing the collective thinking of a significant section of Millennials.

Flexibility for Millennials

Millennials love their freedom. And if there is an option to do it the way they want, it is best for them. They choose the work, time, place and also the employer and are in total control of their lives. Moreover, for someone high on work life balance, this is an ideal situation to be in.

Higher Engagement

When someone has the choice of doing something they like, they normally do the same with passion. Having chosen the kind of work they want to do, they demonstrate high degree of commitment and fire power. This high engagement leads to high quality output. Unlike a job, they also understand each project is like making a jewel. The more finesse and polish they apply, the better will be quality. As their survival depends on it, they give their best. The need for a repeat buyer all the time is very high with this community. Gig workers are tested all the time unlike a stable job with a firm.

Opportunity to Earn More

If you are a salaried employee, you have a fixed salary till the next increment. In a gig economy, if you're good at what you do, you will always be in demand by multiple clients and this obviously enhances your opportunity to make more money than the fixed income group.

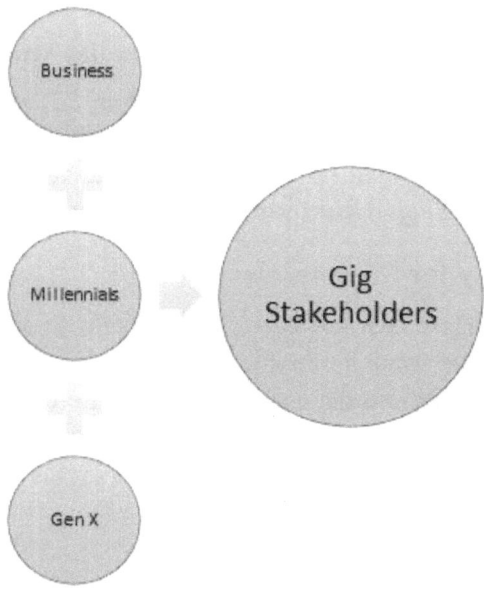

Win – Win for All

For Gen X in This Gig Economy

Gen X, lot of times find themselves unfavourably positioned in the growing gig economy. Unfavourable because they don't really plan to be part of the gig world, yet by default they get into it.

> Mostly Gen X becomes a part of gig world by default and hence find it challenging

Since they plan a linear career for themselves, they do not know what to do in case of career breakdown and find this change very difficult to manage.

Know where to position your next move

They try to work out their own coping mechanisms which neither kick-start their 2nd innings in an engaging way nor they bring in the financial rewards equal to their expertise.

Many of those with whom I have been interacting from Gen X, felt a host of personal, social, and economic anxieties without the cover and support of a traditional employer.

Gig economy provides a platform for Gen X. The platform is loosely structured, the rules of the game are not clearly defined and it is getting increasingly competitive. It can be looked as glass half full or half empty. Gen X may like to read this situation to their advantage and define some rules for their work and thrive in this chaos. After all, experience brings in wisdom and insights. Qualities to deliver this will be Speed, Flexibility and being Inventive.

Leading an enriching life in gig economy is to create a balance between **resourcefulness, purposefulness and feasibility.** In the chaotic 21st century, gig economy is an increasing reality. Gig workers are expected to contribute certain value to the business and it is this value creation which becomes sole survival factor for the warriors.

21st century is a century of paradox. As the world shuts down due to a virus pandemic, it has opened many possibilities and career is one of them. The next chapter explores the career options.

Chapter 7

Case 7

Sridhar is the head of a recruitment team for a large Indian conglomerate. The chairman of the company had created two task forces, one was to recommend which jobs can be automated and handled remotely and the other taskforce was to make recommendations on recruitment strategy for the year. Sridhar was heading the second taskforce on recruitment strategy in the wake of the pandemic.

Sridhar opened the meeting with his colleagues who were representing different functions of the business. He went to the white board and wrote down "In the wake of a pandemic, what skills and competencies will be most relevant for the next few years. The second question was which streams/colleges/institutions one should visit for campus hiring".

The group started deliberating and Sridhar saw two distinct trends. One was championing the old model of hiring engineers plus MBAs from premier institutes. They highlighted the rigor and quality of mind they would bring to the business. However, there was a very vocal second group who were championing the cause of mavericks as fresher's who had entrepreneurial background and were risk takers and came from any stream/background/institutes. Both the cases had their own pros and cons.

Sridhar was facing a deadlock and did not know how to proceed ahead. After a two-hour discussion he called for a lunch break and asked the participants to reconvene later.

Q1) Which group you agree with and why?

Q2) If you were Sridhar, which strategy you would finally recommend?

CAREERS IN THIS MILLENNIUM

This chapter highlights the existing career opportunities along with emerging ones. The opportunities provide a new road map to both Gen X and millennials. The rules of the games are changing. In some new careers, the requirement is very different from the conventional careers as also the road to reach there.

When Gen X started to work, the safe haven with respect to career was either Doctor, Engineer or Chartered Accountant. Civil Services would top the chart and was meant for privileged few with long queue of hopefuls and was highly competitive. Journalism & Advertising were getting defined as structured specialisation, providing some level of Knowledge and training. Functional specialisation was emerging and MBAs were a ticket to corporate career. Hotel Management as a default career for those who didn't find passage in the mainstream. IT was meant to change lives and there were many who wanted to ride that bus. NIIT, Aptech made big fortunes through their educational institutes.

How it has changed in the 21ˢᵗ century?

Come 21ˢᵗ century, the world opened up through internet as never before. Today grandma's bedside story finds great opportunity for monetisation. It's a very different millennium. If you are street smart, you can create value for your products and services and people are willing to pay for it as they see value in it. Let me give an example, there are apps for residential colonies which have a feature of a neighbourhood chef. So if you are fond of cooking, you can commercialise your food. For buyers, it is a win-win, as you get home made food at a lesser price than the restaurant and it eliminates the hassle of cooking on a busy working day. One does not have to stay under a corporate umbrella to do all this.

This is an age of the super specialist, the specialist and the humanist and that's your most important pedigree. Your skill is your qualification. You don't have to exhibit your photos in a photo exhibition to make a fortune, as long as you know how to click well and have a story to tell, a digital gallery will suffice.

Age of Super specialists, Specialists and Humanist

21st century presents us a business paradox, where the big have grown bigger and the self-employed are emerging stronger. The mid-level businesses are increasingly getting consolidated on either side of the value chain. Careers that are shaping up in the present times do not come with a retirement date. With average life expectancy moving up and increasing specialisation, people are more resourceful, dynamic and everlasting.

In the past, Gen X saw some careers getting over even before they even realised it's not there. Undermentioned are some.

Careers With an Obituary Note:

Steno-Typist, Postman, Computer Operator, Video Librarian, Telephone Operator, Photo Studio professionals, General Clerks, Office Manager etc.

These careers have become extinct. Today nobody plans their careers for these kind of jobs. These careers started losing significance as technology started entering our life. The machine could do most of the work done by them. If someone was required to monitor attendance, it became redundant as today you can monitor attendance remotely. There are apps which are connected to GPS and can tell you the exact location of the sales personnel out on a sales call.

With the advent of Artificial Intelligence, Machine Learning, Data Science and Robotics, there are more careers which may be trashed. Technology has started performing the second level of jobs which are beyond the repetitive, routine, monotonous jobs. They are thinking like human brain and delivering the next level of solution.

Careers Going to the Dustbin:

These careers are no more that significant in the present era. To name a few, these are HR administrator, Cashiers, Printing & Publishing, Telemarketers, Recruiters, Travel agents, Accountants, Conventional Soldiers, Stock brokers, Mortgage brokers, Non-Revenue Managers, Broadcasters, IT Support, Financial Planners, Door to Door Sales people, Routine Architects.

Let's look at a telemarketer's job, they make calls, these calls can be made today by an AI based software. Travel agents' numbers are decreasing as intelligent portals are suggesting which holidays to take, how to go, where to stay etc. Any non-revenue earning manager job will fade as the businesses are getting sharper, redefining performance parameter linked to clients, revenue, profits and productivity. Financial planning one of the key jobs in Finance department may soon be replaced by an app which does all your planning anticipating company's intervening variables with ease earlier done by an expert finance professional.

Door to door sales is already getting replaced by digital buying. Demand remains the same, just that the selling place has shifted. A lot of routine architect's job will be replaced by an engineer or non-qualified specialists on sheer pricing. Broadcasters demand is coming down as habits shift towards streaming. With increasing cloud cover to IT systems, the always busy IT support staff may find itself out of favour soon. All the brokers jobs are getting reduced like mortgage, real estate, share market. Intelligent platforms are providing solutions. They are more expansive, analytical and in-depth.

A Recruiters job is threatened by a robot, who can do 1ˢᵗ level of screening and also conduct technical round of interview.

Role of Automation in Shaping Professional Destiny

Automation enabled by technologies including robotics and artificial intelligence brings higher productivity, economic growth, increased efficiencies, safety, and convenience. But these technologies also raise difficult issues in the society about employment, maturity of the alternates and skill readiness and maturity of society to embrace it.

What all can be digitized?

Core Information: Digitization of assets, including infrastructure, connected machines, data, and data platforms.

Operating Process: Digitization of operations, processes, payments and business models & customer and supply chain interactions.

Digitization of the Workforce: Workmen use of digital tools, digitally skilled workforce, and new digital jobs and careers

McKinsey finds that about 60 percent of all occupations have at least 30 percent of activities with the possibility of automation, based on currently demonstrated technologies. This means that most occupations will change, and more & more people will have to work with technology. Highly skilled workers working with technology will benefit.

On a global scale, they calculate that the adaptation of currently demonstrated automation technologies may impact 50% of world economy, or 1.2 billion employees and $14.6 trillion in wages. Just four countries—China, India, Japan, and the United States—account for just over half of these total.

However, all this will also depend on political & socio-economic factors. Whether the companies have that kind of money to invest in technology, what if they get workforce cheaper than technology cost or the politics of masses and stalling any major automation.

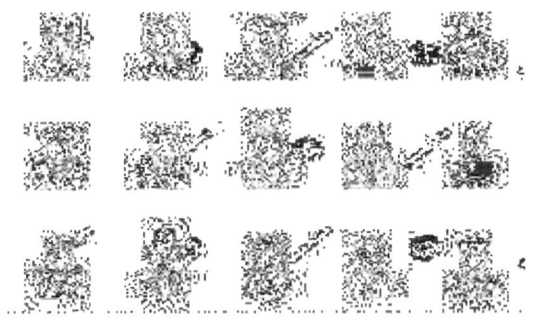

What Are the Emerging Careers?

What are some of the current big tickets in this Millennium? Environment, climate Change, digital technology & automation, increased humanism, digital Entertainment, health, fitness & gig economy. The new & emerging careers are addressing this new world priority.

So we have a Mechatronics Engineer, a combination of mechanical & electronics fields replacing the traditional mechanical engineer and driving automation in manufacturing sector or an Environment Engineer addressing the environmental concern in a project or a Happiness Manager promoting positive emotions at workplace. For digital entertainment there are specialists who are Content Curators focussing on collecting content. A Bio Scientist is continuously looking at alternatives to replace the hazardous plastic. While a Life Coach is working to remove toxic emotions of the coachee.

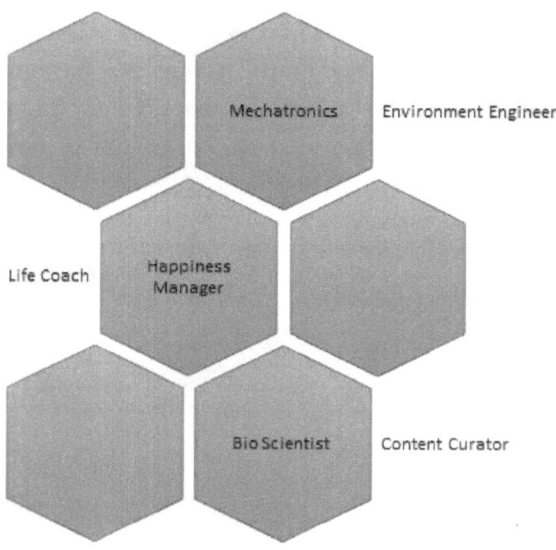

LinkedIn, highlighted the 'Top 15 Emerging Jobs in India for 2020' some of which have been shared below. With over half a billion internet subscribers, according to a McKinsey Report, India is the second fastest digitizing economy in the world. These technological shifts across sectors are sparking the need for new capability building and giving rise to new job roles.

Block chain Developer, Artificial Intelligence Specialist, and JavaScript Developer take the Top 3 spots on the Emerging Jobs list for India in 2020. While tech jobs lead the list, non-tech jobs such as Customer Success Specialist, Digital Marketing Specialist, and Lead Generation Specialist have also seen a significant rise on this year's list.

Businesses also realise that as technology makes deep inroads into the way business is done, the human side may get impacted negatively hence we need a renewed vigour to nourish that. So humanists are back and

> Human side may get impacted negatively because of technology

that's where liberal art is emerging as an alternative education stream as different from Engineers and CAs. Having good human values, nurturing soft skill is as important as a techie job. So, a People Manager or a Customer Relation Manager remains very relevant.

Emergence of Liberal Arts in the Corporate Realm for Certain Jobs

Corporates are preferring to recruit for certain functions, candidates with liberal arts background along with MBA. There is a growing view that engineers are not well trained in life skills. Liberal arts in the not so recent past used to be a profession for the purist. They would pursue careers in academics, research, archaeology, linguistics etc. Knowledge for the sake of knowledge was the driving force. In today's time there is a relevance to their pursuits for businesses and people at large.

A liberal arts programme is based on multiple disciplines and this trains the mind to develop lateral thinking. Along with this, the interactive classes facilitate a spirit of inquiry, critical thinking and open ended analysis as well as verbal and written communication skills in students.

Live cases & field trips, presentations, movies and on-the-job assignments are some of the ways in which students are exposed to multiple facets of an issue and develop life skills which otherwise is missing in the formatted education system. The core of liberal arts is embedded in humanism.

Fields such as civil services, consulting, media, advertising, sales, public relations, research, teaching, banking and the social sector offer promising prospects for liberal arts graduates. Entrepreneurship is also a great possibility.

Careers in Gig Economy

Gig economy provides you with independence, flexibility and the millennials grab it with both hands. It offers you short term projects and there is a section in today's workforce, this is a preferred option. As discussed in the earlier chapter, it also works well with the businesses.

While the context of gig economy is dynamic and evolving, what appears fairly certain is that traditional businesses will continue offloading risk to the individual wherever it can in a disruptive and uncertain economy. It's also similarly certain that temporary contract work will continue to grow as traditional jobs with benefits and salaries will not be cost effective and will start declining. But where does this lead us?

This should lead the economy to open common networks in large sectors, to encourage innovation and independence within the knowledge workers & self-employed in an otherwise insecure world. Transaction-oriented work has already gathered tremendous steam, which suggests that in the not-too-far-off future we'll see an economy that has rebuilt itself on millions of self-employed entrepreneur rather than millions of Nine-to-five jobs. Then for that time, the "gig economy" will just be "the economy."

It is very important to mention here that in gig economy education qualification is not as relevant as it used to be in the past. You may be a 10th graduate and still can be a very successful techie or Java developer. What your buyer values is what value and services you can bring to the platform and not your education. So a YouTuber makes mega bucks and nobody cares about the person's background.

In Conclusion

While the conventional jobs like Sales, Operations, Journalism, Advertising, Civil Services remains, the 21st century with its advancement in science & technology has created immense possibilities for new careers. The question to answer: Is our education system ready to train people in attitude, skills in this rapidly changing world scenario? What change management practises the society must implement to maximise these opportunities?

Below Is an Indicative List of Emerging New Careers:

From Liberal world	From Techie world	From Corporate
Blogger – travel, fashion, food, fiction, photography	Gaming specialist, Business intelligence, Robotic process automation, Data scientist	Bio manufacturing specialist, Biomedical engineer, Biochemist
Writer	Cloud engineer	Medical scientist
Content writer	Machine learning, Artificial Intelligence, Block chain specialist	Mechatronics engineer
Trainer – personal fitness, health, dance, life skills	Network analyst, Backend developer, Full stack engineer	Environment engineer
Coach – life coach, career coach, counsellor, online tutor	Cyber investigator, Cyber security, Computer vision engineer	Portfolio manager
Dietician, yoga teacher	Graphic designer, web designer	Lead generation specialist
Image consulting/Personal styling	Deep learning and AI developer	Business analyst
Fashion design	Virtual and Augmented reality developer	Fashion technologist
Textile and Apparel design	Java developer	
Accessory/Jewellery design	Ethical hacker	
Social media manager/digital marketing, Instagram marketer		
User, tester		
Critic – Movies, Songs, You Tube		
Virtual assistant		

Chapter 8

Case 8

David has been hiding himself in his home for close to 4 months now. After his wife and grownup kids go to work and colleges respectively he picks up the phone to follow up with the search consultants. The answer does not change from the previous day as they say that as soon as they hear something suitable for him they will share. After this he would go to the job search portals and apply online. For weeks, he would not speak to his relatives or friends. Apart from consultants the only other communication in David's life is with his family.

With each passing month David's confidence was going down. And hope was being fast replaced by self-doubt. He was irritable and would pick up fights with his spouse and kids for trivial reasons. He had stopped going out of his house, not even for his morning walks.

David was benched after 22 years in the business world. It was a very cut and dry separation. The business was downsizing and he was given three months' salary cheque along with his separation letter. After serving the organization for such a long time it was the last thing he anticipated. He had big financial commitments including his home loan EMI, kids' education and he was the primary earning member of the house.

Q1: If you were David how would you plan for this phase of your life?

Q2: How should David's family and friends support him in this situation?

GEN X IN THEIR 2ND INNINGS: THE CHALLENGES

It is said that every career experiences two major crashes over a span of 35 to 40 years. They come subtly and the career crashes and after a while it again takes off. This chapter is being written to highlight this phenomenon in the career of Gen X. This generation is more vulnerable than others to experience a career setback in this millennium. Hopefully it triggers a thought process towards change and reinvention.

The 2000s are an interesting millennium; 21st century truly represents a planet based on disruptions. COVID-19 has wreaked havoc in the world and the beauty of nature was missed by most of human population, as they stayed indoors and locked down for months.

> People No More Retire at Age 58, They Are Made to Retire Early or They Plan to Never Retire.

In this millennium, the business reorganises, shuts down, gets acquired overnight. Hate to say this, but jobs get impacted - pink slips, garden leaves is a much bigger phenomenon in this century than ever before.

So Why the 2nd Innings?

Research shows that a professional is at a high risk of losing their job after they cross a threshold of 20 years of work experience. Currently Gen X occupies that space.

The job loss happens primarily for the undermentioned reasons:

1. Less costly resource for same job

2. Volatility of business environment (Reduce Costs)

3. Emergence of Gig workers

4. General management skills of Senior Executives

5. Technology doing human jobs

Job Loss Reasons

The same job can be done by someone younger with lesser pay than present role holder with hefty pay packets. For example, while there are Vice Presidents (normally a N - 2 position) in their late 40s or 50s working with corporate houses, seeing the current hiring trends, the recruitment happens for the same position with candidates in late 30s or early 40s.

Be it business realignment, performance issues or any other, there is a growing trend of redundancies happening post 18-20 years of service in an average career.

Businesses are continuously redefining themselves and cost reduction and increasing efficiency are constant goals for them. Manpower rightsizing is one of the responses.

Gig workers emerge as an option (discussed in detail in Chapter 6) as it is an expertise based service available at a much lower cost if we do an annualised calculation.

As one climbs the corporate ladder, general management competencies get consolidated. People management, process management, reports, reviews, analytics, quality and defects are some examples of the jobs that senior executives do. They become experts in doing this over and over again and miss the trick of making themselves future ready.

Also with technology taking over many human functions, the redundancies are bound to happen.

The Mid-Career Crisis

For Gen X, it is a mid-career crisis. A crisis partly created by business and partly by self.

Role of
Self

Career
Crisis

Role of
Business

While they have served senior positions in the business world, they are increasingly faced with diminishing returns in their mid-career. Here opportunities for new jobs reduces or pay keeps shrinking. Redundancies add to it like icing on the cake.

This crisis comes with a loss of financial strength, lowered self-esteem and social powerlessness

The 'holding environment' of physical, social and psychological space of the corporate life is gone. All in all, a recipe for the incumbent to either become a recluse or reinvent. Ones with tough minds reinvent, most survive with half-hearted attempts.

A mid-career crisis brings in self-doubt i.e. thoughts such as am I good enough? Am I out of the race and youngsters have taken over? Apart from diminished financial returns it also brings in loss of prestige. You had a big team, plush office, so many adjuncts to take care of your other needs. You were in a position of authority, earned respect, instilled awe and fear in juniors who reached out to you. Suddenly all these vanish.

There is a new world where you stand all alone and do not really know what's next for you. And you do not know how to cope with that psychologically.

Most people externalise job loss by citing office politics, bad managers, bad HR practices. However, there is a minority who know in their heart that they could not cope up with the changing times. Yes, they acknowledge their inability to self-develop.

Changing Self for the Changing World

As the world is rapidly changing so is the need to change one's own self. In a business world, what matters is performance on the job, promotion, increment and that's it. Future is what present is showing and nothing more. But this future is short term. If I manage my stakeholders well and show results, I will earn my promotion is *the future* Senior Executives plan for.

While they may visualise how the business will change in future, how markets will shift, how technology will take over human interface they are unable to visualise what they need to do to remain relevant in the future.

It's like the monkey story, you cannot use the same trick to handle a new set of monkeys. You need to learn new tricks to handle a new set of monkeys each time in a new situation.

Reskilling Ahead of Time Is 'in' Time

As one climbs the corporate ladder, general management competencies get consolidated as that is what one masters. They become experts in doing this over and over again and miss the trick of making themselves future proof.

Let me give few examples to highlight the same: say one is a Supply Chain Head, while he manages the supply chain network effectively, he can have an expertise on freights & duties or road transport or shipping. Another example, an HR Head will have general HR management competency but they may like to develop expertise on digital HR platforms or coaching and facilitation or a Finance Head championing borrowings from a lending institution and organising funds at the push of a button.

Identify the Core

It's very important for professionals to identify couple of core areas which can be developed into expertise over a period of time and can be very useful in the 2nd innings. Say a finance professional can become an expert in taxation or bank liaison, or operations professional can develop expertise around production planning, lean management etc., similarly HR person masters coaching or C level search.

Each senior executive representing different functions must plan for the 2nd innings by identifying their core areas and start mastering the same.

If someone has built a huge network of relations over a fairly long career, how they can nurture and further develop that network and make it their expertise.

Leveraging Digital Platforms

Gen X has to make friends with the digital world. Digital platform is the current operating medium. A lot of gig working is happening on the digital platforms. Whether its ERP based platforms or stand-alone app based solutions, they must be comfortable using it.

There is no harm going to a youngster and learning from them. All work related transaction has shifted to online platforms. Even the traditional recruitment consultant is asking candidates to register on a portal.

Activating the Network

It is very important to reach out to your network in case you are at a crossroad in your mid-career. They may not get you a job or have answers for all your questions but they may connect you to someone who has. Primary network to secondary network to tertiary, who knows where it works. Reach out to people and they will reach out to you. Remember the 'law of attraction'.

While Networking works better than going to search consultants or job sites, it is not so popular. Research shows that senior executives hesitate to tap the network either for reasons of vanity or awkwardness about what will others think of them.

I have spoken to many senior executives who find it extremely challenging to reach out to others. They are in a 'denial' mode and falsely believe that others will not understand their true worth or they are still powerful enough for things to happen on its own. But nothing happens on its own.

Secondly they think that time frame to convert through networking is uncertain. So they duck it and approach consultants and recruitment portals in their quest for a quick job.

Being Visible:

It is important to have a point of view and be socially relevant. Unlike the times when Gen X started, the world views were then expressed by Politicians, Journalists, Writers and Celebrities for people at large but today everyone can express their perspective through the platforms of Social Media: Facebook, LinkedIn, Twitter, Instagram.

Social visibility is a constant reminder to the rest of the world that one is agile, connected and has a perspective. It is also important to understand how you want others to know you. Do you want people to know you as the one posting selfies, wishing birthdays & anniversaries to family members on social media or sharing thought provoking perspective?

Developing a change responsive mind-set, upskilling/ reskilling, building core areas, using the digital world, networking and being visible are some of the significant tools for Gen X while they play their 2ⁿᵈ innings.

Chapter 9

Case 9

Sumit had worked hard for his HR brand launch campaign. This campaign was planned as a prelude to the recruitment drive which they were to launch soon in different metros to hire sales force.

He did all that he had learnt over years. He picked up the naukri.com database and sent mailers to prospective candidates. He ran a poster campaign in all institutes and colleges across cities. He also called few placements officers he knew.

Sumit hoped what they did in the past would work this time also. He forgot that the Sales Head had slightly tweaked hiring criteria. They now looked for minimum 1 year of experience.

The recruitment drive failed. They got much smaller presence of candidate in each centre and most of them failed the criteria. His Sales head was livid, he wanted to know why Sumit didn't get the numbers.

Q1: What went wrong with Sumit's HR launch campaign?

Q2: What more Sumit should have done?

WORKING IN 21ST CENTURY

The deserted roads, haunted cities, gives one a feel that they are almost out of a movie scene from 'Legend'. Today it is a living reality. Doors and windows of the world have been shut and everyone literally is indoors warding off the deadly and contagious Coronavirus. The world is locked down, no matter what progress one has made in science & technology, healthcare, space research, oceanography or nuclear physics. It has no answer to the virus as of now. Welcome to 21st century. Volatile, Unpredictable, Complex and Ambiguous.

What is happening to the world because of this pandemic is unprecedented and will have a far and wide impact on globalisation, trade and commerce and glorified capitalism.

This is the battlefield where one has to work. This is a very different karma bhoomi.

Working in a way defines our identity. It can be jobs with large corporate or self-employment. For most they serve as an anchor which roots them to a role, money and to a status. It provides us a format around which we organise our lives, personal goals, leisure and other significant decisions.

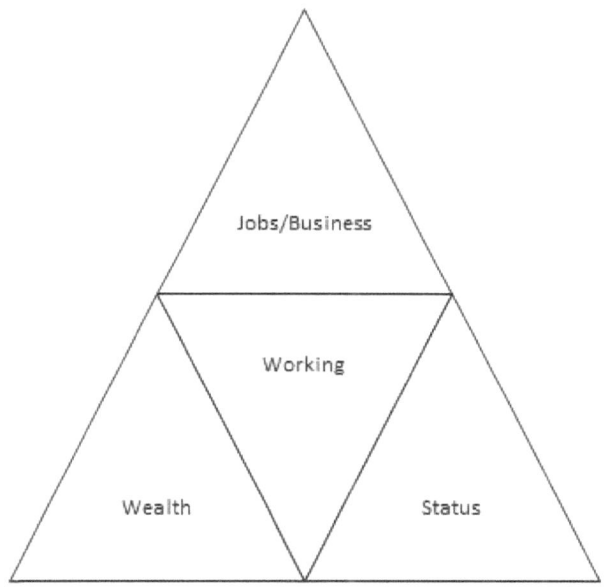

What a Job defines

21ˢᵗ century provides a unique opportunity for real time out of the box options while conventional jobs continue as routine. This chapter is in the context of work engagement for white collar professionals. You can work for a business or you can work for self. You can never retire if you want to or you can retire much ahead of time and still have enough finances to fund rest of your life. It's a world of endless possibilities.

In parallel, there is a dark side - a volatile business environment, threats to human race, fatigue and burn out due to the fast pace of life and disruptive world.

So how should Gen X, Y, Millennials make 21ˢᵗ century work for them?

Attitude Will Be Key

Yet instinctively, humans give their best response when they see possibilities or feel threatened. That's where emotion, mind and soul come together to create a 'never say die belief'. A mind-set which practises mobility and flexibility on a continuous basis. Flexible to shift ideas and accept another point of view, mobile to go places and work there.

Resilient attitude will help them to bounce back and survive an unpredictable world. A strong mind to step out of comfort zone and experience the unknown is the key mantra for the professionals. While formats will be there for conformists but risk takers will have higher success quotient.

Call it a mind of cynic or whatever, after the 2020 pandemic, nothing will be taken at face value, critiquing will emerge as a key mental quality. All ideas will need deep critical thinking and professionals with such abilities will be encouraged. A 360-degree approach to solutioning will be the way to go.

360-degree approach to solutions

Quarantine Only for Self-Development

Learning on a continuous basis is a must in this millennium. It doesn't stop with your education. If you do not want to get redundant, keep upskilling, reskilling. So while you work, keep identifying emerging trends in work, some new benchmark that is being practised elsewhere, do your gap analysis and plunge into the journey of reinvention.

It will be important to insulate yourself from worldly pleasures and take time off for learning on time to time basis.

And this should be a continuous process. Say in Organisation Development different approaches like gestalt, appreciative enquiry, systems thinking or design thinking kept emerging and a good practitioner kept in touch with all the new developments. In this example the change took place over decades but in this century, changes happen very fast maybe over months, year and not decades.

Apart from communication, leadership some of the mandatory generic skills are information literacy, media literacy, technology literacy. A must for all 21st century professionals.

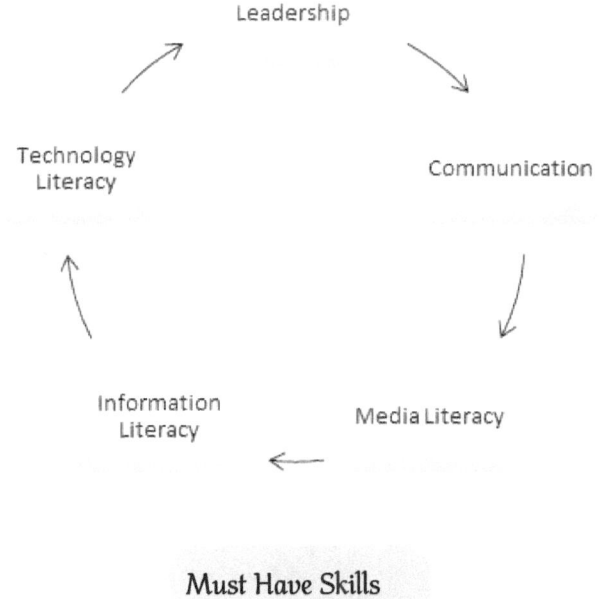

Must Have Skills

Being Clear About Choices

This century experiences fast paced change in success paradigms. If you have mastered your skill over a territory, then create your expertise on the product prototypes, new forms of supply chain etc. As success milestones change so will the means and ways of reaching them. But one needs to be very clear about which route one wants to travel.

The only way to master ambiguity is to be clear about the choices you make. It's like driving through fog, you are more sure if you are driving at a minimal speed on one side of the road and not in the centre. The edge of the road gives you concrete direction about your forward movement.

> The only way to master ambiguity is to be clear about the choices you make

In a crowd of multiple options to choose from, pick up few options in which you are an expert and which are futuristic in nature. Create your professional brand around that.

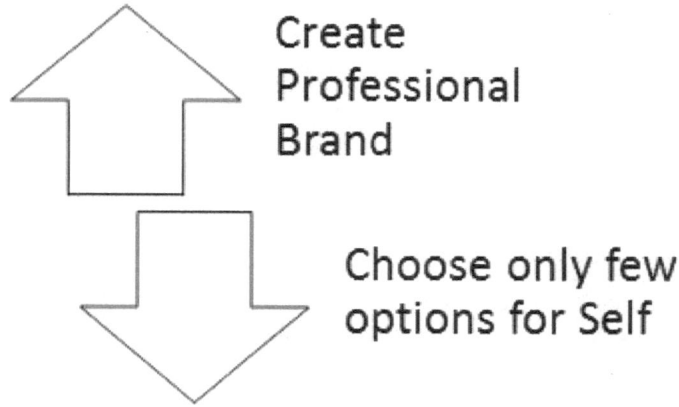

Create Professional Brand

Choose only few options for Self

Redundancies happen most where one is unable to build a bridge between our present and future. Successful professionals make list of future readiness. Let me give an example to highlight. A hotelier was making shift to BPO industry in the early 2000 because the skills were transferrable. But the person was ambitious and an emerging leader. So in his notice period, he developed high level excel skills. So when he joined, he was ahead of the curve. He was self-reliant, second he could do the analytics himself, a must for BPO managers. He made himself future ready. Professionals must not only be clear about their present choices but should also evaluate its future relevance.

Learning Social Skills Yet Again

Social skills are getting replaced by digital protocols and email etiquettes. I remember in the late 90s when mobile phones started entering the working professionals lives. A senior VP rejoiced then saying it is so easy to greet so many at the same time through an sms during Diwali, wow what technology. I thought will he stop going to his close ones? But as it emerged, today I see that it was the beginning of the end of the warm personalised social greetings.

Whether its networking or professional camaraderie the best memories are created when you meet up, when there is a verbal greeting and when people experience you in flesh and blood and not with a digital emoji.

> All Generations must look beyond WhatsApp

Building a Core Group of Relations Beyond Family

I keep mentioning this, it is ultimately good relations that you have invested in that make you go through tough times and not your money. While family still survives as a unit but rest of the relations are gradually moving online. In a digital world, the relations are increasingly getting reduced to cosmetic touch and feel. It's here you have to step out of your comfort zone and reach out, meet up as in the old world. The touch and feel of face to face meeting is any day powerful than Facebook chat.

Nurture Relations

Can I say at all times I have more than 8 to 10 good, reliable relations who will endure through time and space in this journey? Trust, empathy, care is key to such relations. One should consciously nurture a good number of healthy, positive relations outside family.

Half Answers Will Not Move You in Your Career

As competition soars, the world of 'if' and 'but' collapses. Theory of probability needs to give a concrete solution out of a series of random events. You may have many conjectures but give only one answer. Right or wrong, half-truths don't fit in, there is no room for romance. One cannot demonstrate doubt and docility. Any less than temerity is mild and meek. Give concrete solution fast and move forward in career and life.

I strongly believe that from chaos emerges order and current times are chaotic so in solutioning one has to be concrete. That's the risk one has to take.

It's a world belonging to tough ones, strong and confident not the mild mannered under confident person next door.

Anticipate and Embrace Change

My last chapter in this series will be on managing change where I highlight and detail why it is difficult to implement changes.

Change is permanent and the ability to see the future and change accordingly is one aspect and the second is to know in the present what has changed from the past and how to cope up with that.

As Bertrand Russel said 'knowledge is power'. It is this power we need to develop our expertise in. Staying ahead or at par with the knowledge curve will be a key in this millennium. Identifying all tools relevant for working professionals, knowing most of the same and mastering some.

Build a Fixed Deposit of Good References

In a closely connected world, businesses reach out to your co-professionals to validate your credentials. Having a good set of references is like having a fixed deposit. You never know when you need to encash it. A good reference is like a last minute glucose boost for you while completing a marathon. They take you across the finish line. That's where your investments in relations take centre stage.

Do you have good, positive, healthy professional relations nurtured over time and emotions. Even if you have moved out of the organisation, have you kept in touch with some key relations. They can be superiors, peers, juniors or direct team members. Keep in touch on a regular basis outside birthday wishes. Send them industry relevant articles, meet them at least twice a year. Create good, positive memories of yourself. In 21st century a good word of mouth is like a gospel from the bible.

> Even if you have moved out of the organisation, have you kept in touch with some key relations?

All that I have talked of here is what I have seen achievers doing day in and day out in the current context. They know and practise these aspects. They understand that there is a thin line separating them from being relevant or fading into oblivion.

Chapter 10

Case 10

Swati and Fatima had a very positive reputation while dealing with employees. They were the star performers of the HR team. Mostly on meeting them, the employees would come out happy and satisfied.

Swati and Fatima's manager was facing a big problem from his star performers as the employee satisfaction dipped. HR had taken the decision of automating all employee grievance handling.

The face to face interaction was reduced to 2 levels of interaction on a digital platform. First level being the chat and the second level was on call. Swati and Fatima instead of taking rounds of the floor were sitting behind their laptops and monitoring employee wellness.

There was a big change in the way they would do their job and they were hating it. They were missing the service levels, not promptly solving the employee queries and updating the call logs. The MIS was showing poor score on employee problem resolution and continuous missing of deadlines on open tickets.

Q1: What should the Manager of Swati and Fatima do?

Q2: What are the few things you suggest to make automation successful in HR?

THE DIFFICULTY IN CHANGING

This is the last chapter in this book. In the earlier chapters, I have discussed many aspects which may require deep personal change. One is good to read and it is another matter to implement. And that is the difficult part.

About 70% of change management initiatives become unsuccessful. Organisations and people practice it for some time and find it easy and convenient to slip back to old habits.

Those who have successfully crossed the boundary say that implementing change requires huge rigour and discipline.

NOT TODAY

Change Is a Personal Choice

Wanting to change is a personal choice and being convinced about the need to change will drive individuals to abandon a defunct behaviour and embrace a new one.

In the lockdown of 2020, people may be doing a lot of stuff, which they may not adapt as a behaviour once the lockdown is over. For them to adapt, they must have a deep desire to change, they must see a value of that doing in their life. They may continue with cooking as they discovered that they enjoyed doing it and got appreciation from others, and it also prepares them for future emergency (pain) or generally as a new hobby (pleasure). Implementing change in life is driven by a desire to enhance pleasure or mitigate pain. Nobody embraces change just like that.

To implement change one needs to be very clear about the gap i.e., what needs to be changed and the desire to really bridge the gap. Being self-aware and knowing what to address is a first concrete step in managing change.

Yet there is more consistency of change initiatives failing than succeeding. People continue to practise the same behaviour and get the same results and do not make the difficult choice.

Fear of Failure

The single most unseen motivation stopping us from implementing change is fear of failure. A generation gap and the father realises he must change to understand his child better. He makes a long list of behaviours that will help him to connect with his child at ground zero level and does nothing after that.

When I asked him about it in my coaching session with him, he said he could not implement. As he was scared of failing, the change was too steep and his family would have made fun of him. So it was best to not try.

People are scared of failing. They are not prepared to lower their guards. They don't want to feel vulnerable in front of others. No school or college curriculum teaches you how to deal with failure. It's a lesson learnt the tough way in life. Lacking in attitude to deal with failure, they do not even attempt, lest they fail.

Unwillingness to Step Out of Comfort Zone

Continuing the father-child example, the father had made the change plan himself. Even if he found it steep, he could have revised it to simplify it. But the effort of implementing change was far too much compared to living with a toxic relation. He was not willing to risk his present for a better future.

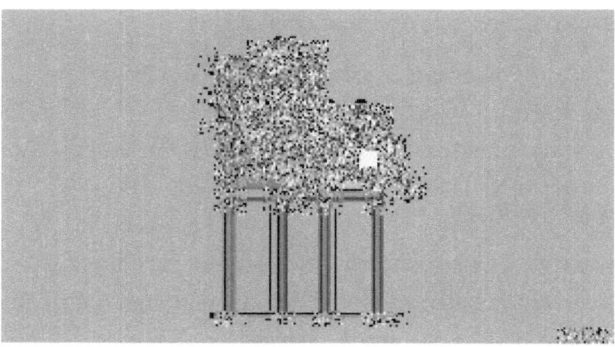

People are unwilling to remove the mask they have put on; they think they will be exposed. So they don't want to try. They are happy where they are.

They want to stay in their comfort zone.

Unable to See the Benefit

'It's my life, why should I change. I am happy the way I am; I don't think any new approach will make things better for me', said a new participant in my coaching program. 'Then why are you here'? I asked. 'My company nominated me,' came the terse reply. I checked again with her, 'these are some development goals jointly agreed between you and your line manager, what do you have to say'? 'Oh that was a discussion I wanted to end fast and I don't see any of these goals benefiting me in the future, will this get me a good increase or promotion'? she retorted.

Then there was a long discussion between me and her to connect it to the big picture and what benefits these development goals can bring in her career.

Lot of times people don't want to change because they don't see the benefit for them. For change to happen, one must not only accept it cognitively but also should be sufficiently emotionally aroused to reach the end goal. They must connect it to the big picture of their life, how will it make their life better and how will they be more effective.

Blocked by Openness

Edward De Bono in his book on 'Lateral Thinking' says that human thinking is unable to adjust to newer options and opportunities for they cannot even see them. People's thinking is primarily driven by past experiences and assumptions. This results in a definite disadvantage for new ideas and seeing emerging patterns. While it helps you to navigate with your current situation, it blocks you in a new changed situation.

> People's thinking is primarily driven by Past Experiences and Assumptions

Mostly change is there even before one realises is a key point. People play the catching up game. Look at the fluid financial situations with some banks, some people anticipated the collapse of a certain bank and removed their funds but majority could not. They are stuck now as the recovery process is painfully slow. For some it was their life savings.

Socio-Religious Impediments

Many a times our religious and community beliefs stop us from changing. Having strong influences in our lives, starting with formative childhood to defined adulthood, the rituals of society define some ways of life and resist any change which threatens that. Say patriarchy still prevalent in the top management in India. It becomes obvious when we see limited representation of woman in the board. God takes care of me and he will continue to do so. So one need not listen to others. But god takes care through people only. These, almost fatalistic assumptions can be big impediments to change.

No Backup Plans

Another reason why personal change fails is because one tries to implement random change plan. It is a linear plan, which means that if this plan fails as the path to change is always a difficult one, there is no Plan B to reach the change goals.

It becomes very easy to abandon the challenging change route in the absence of concrete alternatives.

> Some Coaches fail to help participants develop alternate back up plan

Managing change means managing personal transition. Managing Change is more conceptual and high level while transition is at the ground level.

Managing Personal Transition

Transition is the personal response to that change. This has an emotional content and it is internal to the person. Normally the first response to change is denial that change has actually happened followed by resistance to change and holding on to past.

Denial

Holding on to Past   Resistance to Change   Push Back

Awareness

Why we resist Change

In most cases of managing transition, people get stuck with denial or resistance. They think what has happened will go away and it is only a temporary phase. And they wait endlessly till they realise it is not going back any longer and the only option is moving forward. For some, it may be too late a response. Change sweeps them over and they are unable to overcome it.

However, a good transition is one when someone is able to move away from denial and resistance at an early stage and is open to explore the new ways of life.

Zone of Control and Influence

The most successful implementation in managing transition to a new behaviour is when you are aware of what you can control and what you cannot control. This makes journey of personal change more easy to undertake. Implementing in steps in areas one can control and preparing a plan to take help for areas one cannot control. The second one is about how you can influence others to help you in your journey. This approach can help them to manage personal change more effectively.

> Awareness of what you can control and what you cannot control

Being Inside Out

'Change, Real Change comes from being Inside Out' says Stephen Covey. To manage any transition for change the approach has to be inside out, coming from within.

No change happens when you wait for others to do something first or the environment to change. Let autumn come I will start my exercises and the autumn comes and goes but exercise never starts.

Any inside out approach is beyond a quick fix and quick heal soap. There is no Santa here, only a strong will and intense desire to change will make it happen. It is working with the root, the basic premise of one's thoughts, values and actions. To merge the rational conscious world, the semi

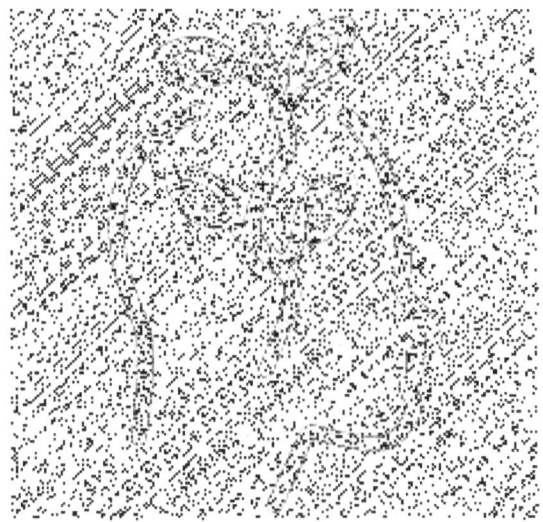

rational subconscious world into one. Your emotions have to be that profound and powerful to make you ready for change.

The problem is people look for an 'outside in' approach. Somebody else will do it for them. The moment we externalise it, we neither have the will nor the energy to run a tough personal change management program. I have already justified to myself that only if someone does it for me, then I will do. How someone else can change your behaviour in adult learning? People don't want to ask this question.

In conclusion, the chapters in this book talks about the understanding of different generations in this millennium. I have also tried to highlight some of the key characteristics of 21st century where change is happening much faster than ever in the history of human civilisation. The key question to ask is how prepared are we to deal with this change. Whether its dealing with different generations, looking at career opportunities, changing work norms and general life approaches. If disruption is a new normal in life, are we the 21st century professionals equipped to deal with it.....

Till again....

REFERENCES

- Deloitte Survey 2019
- Gallup Survey on Millennials
- PWC Report
- Forbes Articles
- LinkedIn Survey December on Hot Jobs

TERMS

Baby Boomers: Covers generation of people born before 1966

Gen X: Covers generation of people born between 1966 to 1980

Millennials or Generation Y: Who reached adulthood in the early 21st century and covers the generation of people born between 1980 and 1994.

Generation Z: As anyone born between 1997 and 2012

VUCA: Volatile, Unpredictable. Complex and Ambiguous

MIS: Management Information System

ESTJ: Extravert, Sensing, Thinking & Judgemental

FOR YOUR JOURNEY......

Your living is determined not so much by what life brings to you as by the attitude you bring to life; not so much by what happens to you as by the way your mind looks at what happens.

Khalil Gibran